# STICKMEN'S GUIDE
# TO YOUR
# BEATING HEART

Thanks to the creative team:
Senior Editor: Alice Peebles
Fact Checking: Kate Mitchell
Design: www.collaborate.agency

Original edition copyright 2017 by Hungry Tomato Ltd.

Hungry Tomato®
A division of Lerner Publishing Group, Inc.
241 First Avenue North
Minneapolis, MN 55401 USA

For reading levels and more information,
look up this title at www.lernerbooks.com.

Main body text set in Avenir Next Medium 9.5/12.
Typeface provided by Linotype AG.

**Library of Congress Cataloging-in-Publication Data**

Names: Farndon, John, author. | Dean, Venitia, 1976- illustrator.
Title: Stickmen's guide to your beating heart / John Farndon ;
illustrated by Venitia Dean.
Other titles: Your beating heart
Description: Minneapolis : Hungry Tomato, [2017] | Series:
Stickmen's guides to your awesome body | Audience: Ages 8-12. |
Audience: Grades 4 to 6. | Includes index.
Identifiers: LCCN 2016046941 (print) | LCCN 2016050331
(ebook) | ISBN 9781512432152 (lb : alk. paper) | ISBN
9781512450149 (eb pdf)
Subjects: LCSH: Heart—Juvenile literature. |
Cardiovascular system—Juvenile literature. | Blood—
Juvenile literature. | CYAC: Circulatory system.
Classification: LCC QP111.6 .F37 2017 (print) | LCC
QP111.6 (ebook) | DDC 612.1/7—dc23

LC record available at https://lccn.loc.gov/2016046941

Manufactured in the United States of America
1-41770-23531-1/11/2017

# STICKMEN'S GUIDE
## TO YOUR
## BEATING HEART

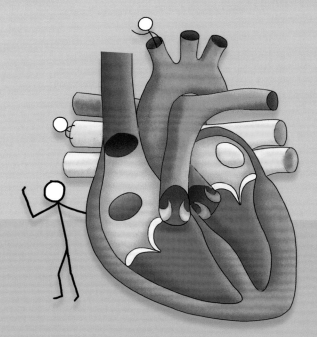

by John Farndon
Illustrated by Venitia Dean

HUNGRY
TOMATO®

Minneapolis

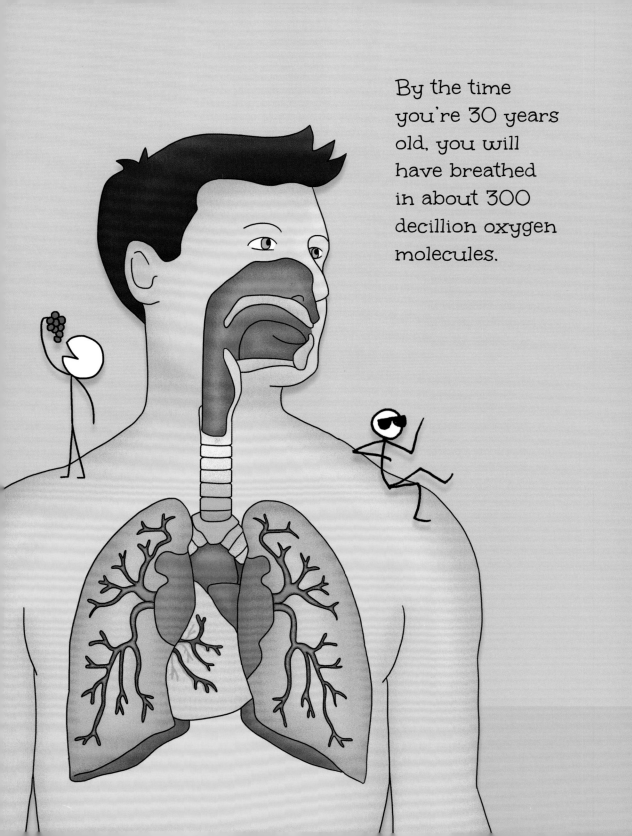

By the time you're 30 years old, you will have breathed in about 300 decillion oxygen molecules.

# Contents

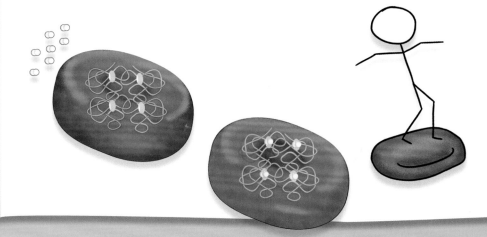

# Your Beating Heart

Every cell in your body needs a nonstop supply of oxygen from the air. Without it, cells in your brain die in minutes! To keep up this vital supply, your body has two interlocking systems. Scientists call them the respiratory and cardiovascular systems—but they just mean breathing and blood circulation.

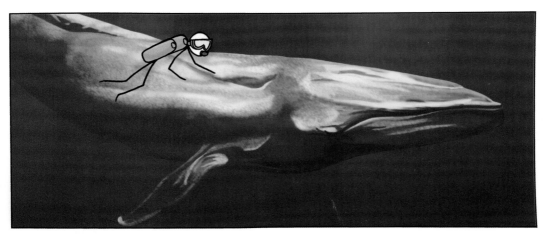

## Big-hearted

The biggest heart in the world belongs to the blue whale. It's about the size of a bumper car at the fair and weighs about 440 pounds (200 kilograms). If you're very small, you might even be able to squeeze inside its main outflow pipe (the aorta) and into the pumping chamber inside! Your heart is about the size of an apple. Yet apart from its size, the whale's heart is pretty much like yours.

## Breathing Air

The average human being breathes in about 145 gallons (550 liters) of oxygen per day. So around the world, people breathe in nearly 1 trillion gallons (4 trillion L) of oxygen. We breathe out about 800 billion gallons (3 trillion L) of carbon dioxide.

## Faint-hearted

Diseases related to the heart are now the biggest cause of early death around the world. And they are going up rapidly. In 1990, over 12 million people died of heart disease. In 2013, it was over 17 million. It is thought that this may be because more people are living to the age when heart disease is a risk.

## Love Hearts

The heart has been associated with love since ancient times. And we often tag Internet posts with a heart symbol. Yet the heart symbol is nothing like the shape of your own heart, which has no particular shape at all. Scholars think the heart symbol was developed in the late Middle Ages.

## Heart Memories

In the past, people thought memories were stored in the heart as well as the brain. And it may be that heart cells have some kind of memory. The evidence is thin, but a few patients who received a heart transplant seemed to develop the same odd tastes in food as the donors who gave them their new hearts.

# Breathing

Your lungs are amazingly good at taking in lots of oxygen from the air every few seconds. The lungs contain a vast network of airways that allows the oxygen you breathe in to pass into the bloodstream, so it can then be carried all around the body.

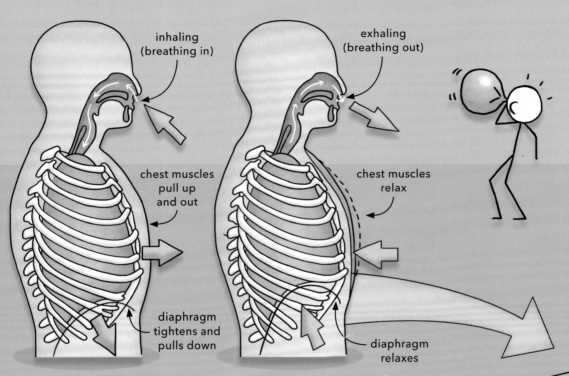

inhaling
(breathing in)

exhaling
(breathing out)

chest muscles
pull up
and out

chest muscles
relax

diaphragm
tightens and
pulls down

diaphragm
relaxes

## Breathe!

Breathing starts with the diaphragm. This is a sheet of muscle that domes up under the lungs. When you breathe in, it tightens and flattens downward, making more space for your lungs. At the same time, muscles between your ribs, known as intercostal muscles, pull your chest out and up. When you breathe out, the opposite happens.

## Air Bags

Your lungs are a pair of organs inside your chest that are filled with tiny branching airways. When you breathe in, air is sucked in through your mouth or nose and rushes down your trachea (the windpipe in your neck). Deep inside your chest, the trachea forks into two airways, or bronchi (plural of bronchus), one leading to each lung. Inside the lungs, the bronchi branch into millions of smaller airways called bronchioles.

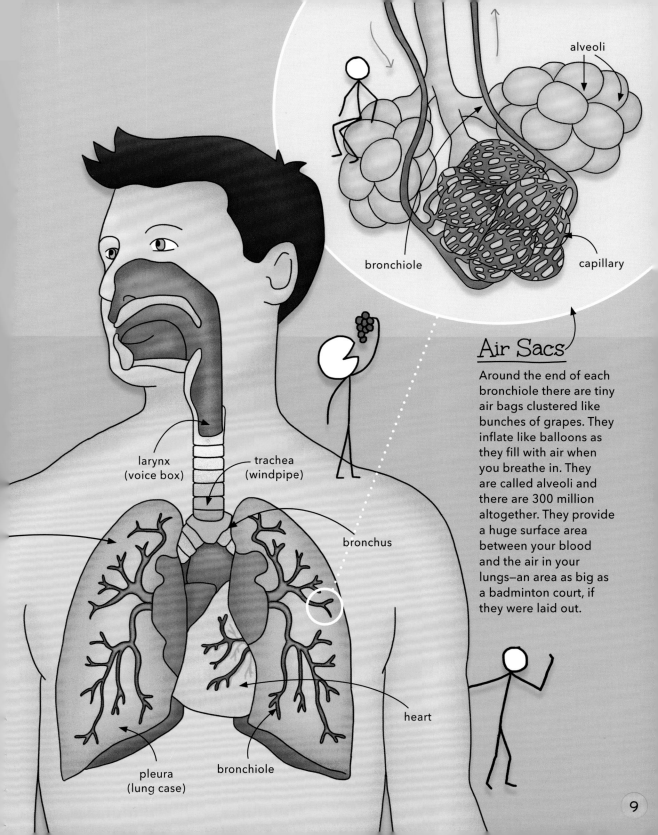

alveoli

bronchiole

capillary

## Air Sacs

Around the end of each bronchiole there are tiny air bags clustered like bunches of grapes. They inflate like balloons as they fill with air when you breathe in. They are called alveoli and there are 300 million altogether. They provide a huge surface area between your blood and the air in your lungs—an area as big as a badminton court, if they were laid out.

larynx
(voice box)

trachea
(windpipe)

bronchus

heart

pleura
(lung case)

bronchiole

# Blood Circulation

Your body cells really need their oxygen, and it's the blood's task to supply it. Pumped by the heart, blood picks up fresh oxygen from your lungs, carries it around the body through a network of pipes, then goes back to the lungs for more. At the same time, it carries waste carbon dioxide to the lungs for breathing out.

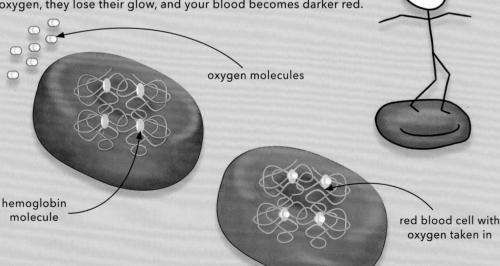

Pulmonary Circulation

right lung

## Two Circulations

The blood circulation is divided into two separate networks that come together in your heart: the pulmonary and systemic. *Pulmonary* means "related to lungs." The pulmonary is just a short network that brings fresh oxygen from your lungs to your heart. The systemic goes around your body. It carries oxygen-rich blood out from the left side of your heart. Then it brings this blood all around the body.

Key     oxygenated blood     deoxygenated blood

## Oxygen Ferries

Oxygen is ferried around the body by 25 trillion button-shaped red blood cells. They contain tangly molecules called hemoglobin. Hemoglobin glows red when it takes on a load of oxygen. That's what makes your blood bright red. Once the cells have delivered their oxygen, they lose their glow, and your blood becomes darker red.

oxygen molecules

hemoglobin molecule

red blood cell with oxygen taken in

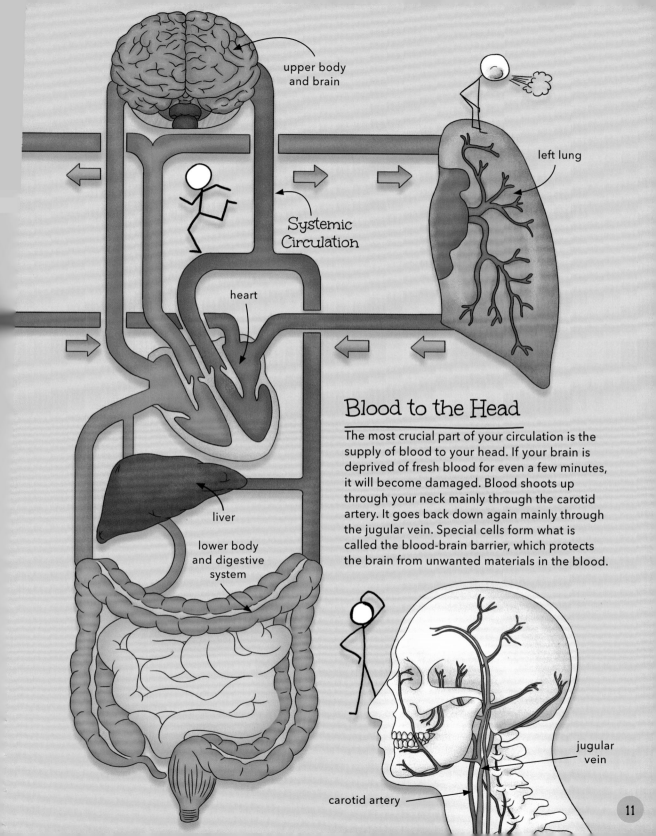

upper body
and brain

left lung

Systemic
Circulation

heart

## Blood to the Head

The most crucial part of your circulation is the
supply of blood to your head. If your brain is
deprived of fresh blood for even a few minutes,
it will become damaged. Blood shoots up
through your neck mainly through the carotid
artery. It goes back down again mainly through
the jugular vein. Special cells form what is
called the blood-brain barrier, which protects
the brain from unwanted materials in the blood.

liver

lower body
and digestive
system

jugular
vein

carotid artery

# Heartbeat

Your heart is an amazing little pump made of pure muscle. Every second of your life, it is squeezing away, pushing blood around your body. It owes its steady beat to the special muscle it is made from, called cardiac muscle, which contracts and relaxes rhythmically by itself.

## Double Heart

Your heart is not just one pump but two, set side by side and separated by a wall of muscle. The left side is stronger, driving oxygen-rich blood all the way around the body. The right sends blood to the lungs and back again. Each side has two chambers, separated by a one-way valve. The atrium at the top is where blood gathers. The ventricle below is the main pumping chamber.

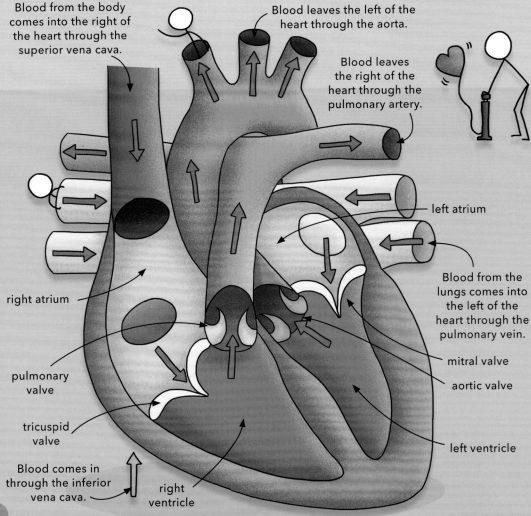

Blood from the body comes into the right of the heart through the superior vena cava.

Blood leaves the left of the heart through the aorta.

Blood leaves the right of the heart through the pulmonary artery.

right atrium

pulmonary valve

tricuspid valve

Blood comes in through the inferior vena cava.

right ventricle

left atrium

Blood from the lungs comes into the left of the heart through the pulmonary vein.

mitral valve

aortic valve

left ventricle

# Heart Cycle

Every time your heart beats, it goes through the same sequence, called the cardiac cycle. This has two phases—systole (contraction) and diastole (relaxation)—that sweep in a wave across the heart. In systole, first the atria (plural of atrium) squeeze to drive blood into the ventricles, then the ventricles squeeze to drive blood out through the arteries. In diastole, first the atria, then the ventricles relax to allow them to fill up again.

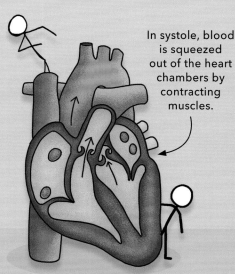

In systole, blood is squeezed out of the heart chambers by contracting muscles.

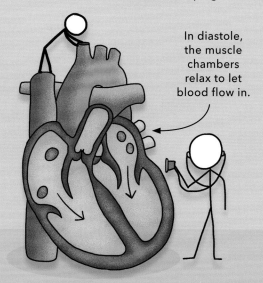

In diastole, the muscle chambers relax to let blood flow in.

# Steady Beat

An electrocardiogram (ECG or EKG) can monitor the heart by picking up the tiny electrical signals it sends out every time it beats. Typically, your heart beats about 75 times a minute. But this can more than double when you exercise hard. The ECG here shows regular spikes for each beat. Erratic spikes show there's a problem with the heart.

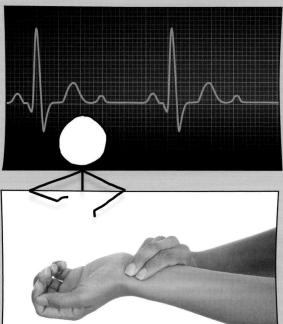

# Feeling Your Pulse

When the valves of the heart snap shut, they send a shock wave or pulse running through your arteries. Doctors can hear this pulse with a special listening device called a stethoscope. You can also feel it yourself by gently laying two fingers on the inside of your wrist, where your radial artery comes close to the surface.

# Arteries and Veins

You have millions of blood vessels—pipes that carry blood—threading through your body. Some are as wide as a pencil. Others are thinner than a hair. The largest blood vessels carrying oxygen-rich blood away from the heart are called arteries. The largest blood vessels carrying oxygen-poor blood back to the heart are called veins.

## Running in Parallel

The body's branching networks of blood vessels are like two intertwined rivers. Throughout the body, bright red arteries carrying blood away from the heart run alongside blue veins carrying it back again. The largest blood vessels are those linked directly to the heart: the ascending and descending aorta (arteries), and the superior and inferior vena cava (veins).

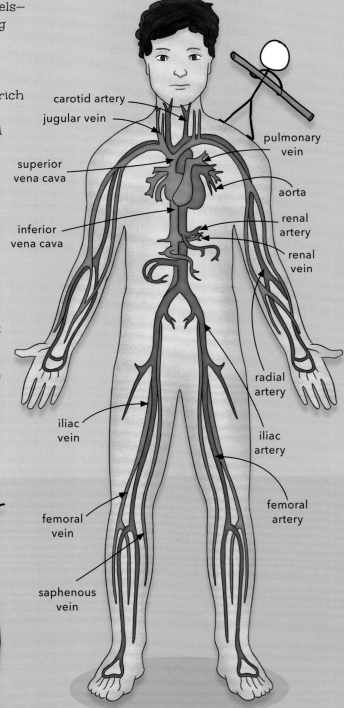

carotid artery

jugular vein

pulmonary vein

superior vena cava

aorta

renal artery

inferior vena cava

renal vein

radial artery

iliac vein

iliac artery

femoral vein

femoral artery

saphenous vein

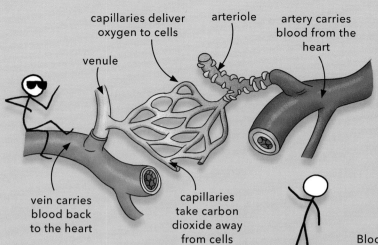

capillaries deliver oxygen to cells

arteriole

artery carries blood from the heart

venule

vein carries blood back to the heart

capillaries take carbon dioxide away from cells

## Branching Pipes

Arteries branch into narrower arterioles, and arterioles branch into even narrower capillaries, where the blood gives up its oxygen to cells. Without oxygen, the blood becomes dark red and is picked up by more capillaries and returned to wider venules, and even wider veins, to make its journey back to the heart.

## Active Pipes

Blood vessels are not simply stiff pipes. They have valves and muscular walls that control the flow of blood. They may widen when you're hot, to allow more blood to get near the surface to cool off, which is why you may look red when you're hot. Or they may narrow when it's cold to keep blood warm inside, which is why you can look white or even blue with cold.

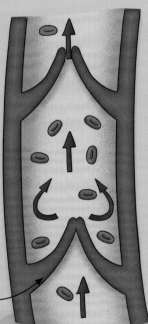

Blood flow in the veins often has to go upward, against gravity.

Valves in the veins open only in one direction.

Valves are pushed close if blood tries to flow back down.

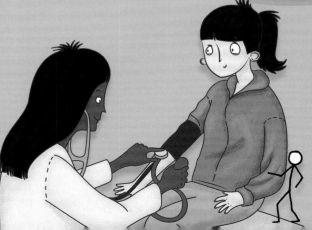

## Under Pressure

The muscles of the walls of blood vessels squeeze or relax to control the pressure of blood. The pressure must be strong enough to push oxygen-rich blood to every cell, yet not so strong that its bursts the delicate capillaries. Doctors can check your blood pressure with a simple cuff that squeezes your arm to reveal how much it affects the blood flow.

# How Cells Breathe

Like a machine, your body cells need a constant supply of fuel to keep them going. Their fuel is glucose, a kind of energy-rich sugar that your body makes by breaking down the food you eat. But just as fire needs air to burn, so your cells need oxygen to use glucose. That's why you need to breathe as well as eat!

## Mini Power Stations

Inside every one of your body cells there are microscopic furnaces called mitochondria (plural of mitochondrion). Mitochondria break down glucose to release tiny bursts of energy with the help of oxygen supplied in your blood. This generates heat, just like a fire. It's called cellular respiration.

Cellular respiration packs energy into millions of tiny molecules of a special chemical called ATP (adenosine triphosphate). The energy is released when needed.

oxygen in

carbon dioxide out

lung

Cell

mitochondria

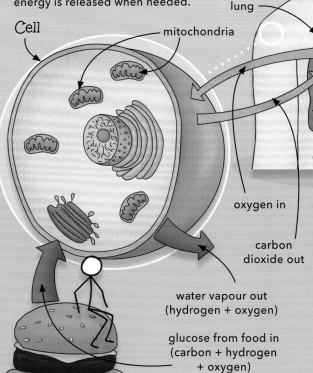

oxygen in

carbon dioxide out

water vapour out
(hydrogen + oxygen)

glucose from food in
(carbon + hydrogen
+ oxygen)

## Sugar Power

Glucose is made mainly from carbon and hydrogen. When your cells break up glucose to release its energy, the hydrogen bonds with oxygen to make water, and the carbon bonds with oxygen to make carbon dioxide. Carbon dioxide is poisonous, so the body must get rid of it. This is what happens when you breathe out.

## Heat Control

For body processes to work well, your body must stay at a steady 37°C (98.6°F). So you have a temperature control in your brain called the hypothalamus to monitor how hot you are. If you're too hot, the hypothalamus tells your body to lose heat by sweating. Sweating takes warm water out of your body and cools your skin as moisture evaporates.

## Too Cold

If you're too cold, the hypothalamus alerts your thyroid, which sends chemical messages to stoke up cellular respiration. It also tells muscles to move rapidly (which is why you shiver) and sends signals to restrict the supply of blood to your skin and cut heat loss.

## We are Family

Mitochondria are almost like independent organisms trapped inside your body cells. The genes of mitochondria are known as mDNA (mitochondrial DNA). They are passed on through mothers for generations. They remain almost unchanged, so using mDNA you can trace your family history far back in time. Amazingly, mDNA shows that we all have very mixed ancestors, no matter where we were born.

# What Is Blood?

Blood might look a little like red ink. But if you viewed it through a powerful microscope, you'd see it has lots of different ingredients. It's full of a whole zoo of different kinds of cells and other ingredients. It is the body's transportation system, carrying not only oxygen to the cells but also food. It helps defend the body against disease too.

## Blood Cells

Your blood is populated by three kinds of cell: platelets, red blood cells, and white blood cells. Red blood cells, or erythrocytes, are button-shaped cells that carry oxygen. White blood cells, also known as leucocytes, are your body's main defense against germs.

### Red Blood Cells

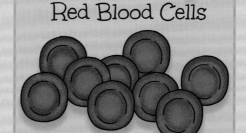

#### Erythrocytes
The body makes 2 million new red blood cells every second. They are much smaller than most white cells.

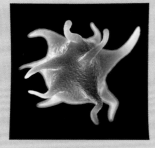

## First Aid Kit

Platelets are the blood's emergency repair team, made of scraps that break off other cells. When you cut yourself, platelets instantly gather to deal with the damage. They send out an alarm in chemicals called clotting factors. These encourage a protein called fibrin to grow and plug the leak. The fibrin dries out to form a scab, protecting the wound until it has healed.

## White Blood Cells

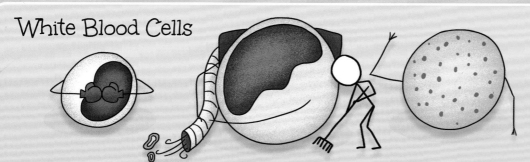

### Lymphocytes
are cells that fight germs. There are at least five different kinds, including B cells, T cells, and Natural Killers.

### Monocytes
are the biggest white blood cells and act like street sweepers, sucking up debris.

### Granulocytes
have colored grains and come in three kinds: neutrophils, eosinophils, and basophils *(right)*.

## The Watery Bit

All the blood's ingredients float in a fluid called plasma. Plasma makes up just over half your blood. It's pale yellow in color and is mostly water, but it also contains many dissolved chemicals, such as salts and glucose, that it brings to your cells for food.

water

salts

proteins

urea (waste)

sugars

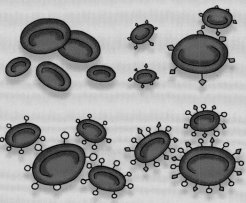

## Your Own Blood

If you have a major operation or a bad accident, you can lose a lot of blood and may need a transfusion, or input, of someone else's blood. But people have blood belonging to one of four different groups: A, B, AB, and O—and they don't mix because your body's immune system will fight against blood from the wrong group. So you must be given the right type.

## How Much Blood Do You Have?

A newborn baby has about the same amount of blood as liquid in a can of soda. By the time you're about eight years old, you have enough blood to fill a 0.5-gallon bottle (2 L). By the time you're an adult, you can fill two or more of these bottles!

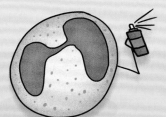

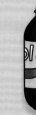

### Neutrophils
are an army of pink-grained cells that fight bacteria and fungi. When they've done their job, they end up as white pus.

### Eosinophils
are a select bunch of peach-grained cells that handle parasites and things you might be allergic to.

### Basophils
are the lookouts, with large blue grains. They react to irritants by sending out a chemical alert called histamine.

# Blood in Action

When your body comes under attack from disease-causing bacteria, viruses, and other germs, it's time for your body to mount a defense. It does this with an array of biological weapons known as the immune system. The most important part of this is your white blood cells.

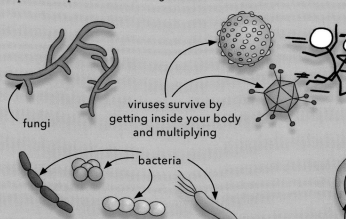

fungi

viruses survive by getting inside your body and multiplying

bacteria

## 1. The Invaders

Germs are tiny organisms that make you sick when they invade or infect your body and multiply. Each kind of germ causes a particular disease. For example, different bacteria cause typhoid, tetanus, or whooping cough. Viruses cause colds, flu, and mumps. Fungi cause conditions such as candida and aspergillosis (often affecting the lungs).

## 2. Germ Swallowers

When germs invade your body, two main kinds of white blood cell go into action to fight them off: phagocytes and lymphocytes. Phagocytes form the first line of defense. Phagocytes swallow invading germs and dissolve them. Once they've swallowed a germ, they display the germ's identity tag or antigen on their outside, identifying them to other immune system cells.

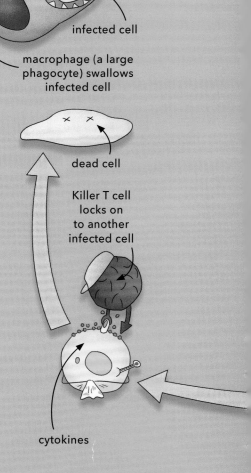

infected cell

macrophage (a large phagocyte) swallows infected cell

dead cell

Killer T cell locks on to another infected cell

cytokines

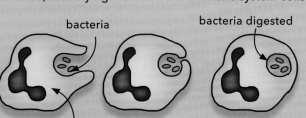

bacteria

bacteria digested

phagocyte

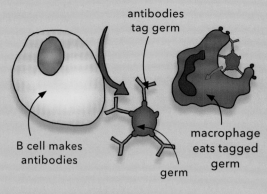

antibodies
tag germ

B cell makes
antibodies

macrophage
eats tagged
germ

germ

## 3. Targeting

Lymphocytes target particular germs. One kind, called B lymphocytes, targets free-roaming germs. Each B lymphocyte has its own antibodies: special chemicals that lock on to a particular germ's antigen. When an antibody meets its antigen, its B lymphocyte makes more antibodies. When they lock on to germs, they make them better targets, especially for extra-large phagocytes called macrophages.

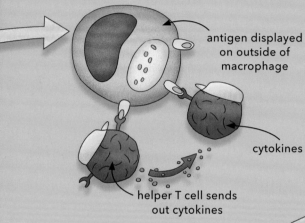

antigen displayed
on outside of
macrophage

cytokines

helper T cell sends
out cytokines

## 4. Beating Viruses

Once viruses invade cells, they are hidden. That's where T lymphocytes come in. Helper T lymphocytes are alerted by telltale signs of damage and also by virus antigens on macrophages that have swallowed invaded cells. They then multiply rapidly and send out alarm chemicals called cytokines. The cytokines activate cells called Killer Ts. Killer T cells target the antigens on other cells, lock on to them, then flood them with toxic chemicals to kill the cell, virus and all.

## 5. Remembering

As lymphocytes identify and attack germs, they make special memory cells. Memory cells hang around long after the battle against the infection is won. So they are on hand to mount a much more rapid and powerful response should the same germs turn up again. Vaccines work by giving you a mild infection of the germ to create memory cells armed and ready for a real attack.

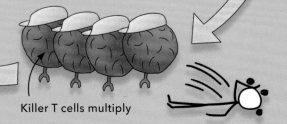

Killer T cells multiply

# Mending Hearts

The heart is an amazing organ that keeps on beating nonstop throughout your whole life. But sometimes, especially later in life, the automatic beating of the heart can go wrong or stop altogether. Fortunately, doctors are finding more and more ways of dealing with heart problems.

## Heart Problems

The heart can suffer in three main ways: heart attack, cardiac arrest, and stroke.

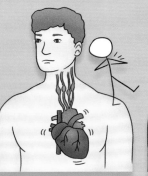
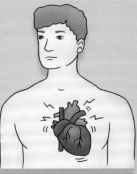
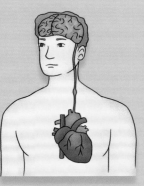

1 In a heart attack, the heart muscle fails because the arteries around the heart become blocked.

2 In cardiac arrest, the heart stops beating because the electrical signals that fire the muscle stop.

3 In a stroke, blood flow to the brain is cut off, often by a blood clot in an artery.

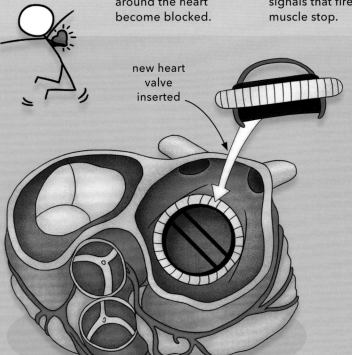

new heart valve inserted

## Heart Valve

Sometimes the valves in the heart can become floppy and fail to shut properly, weakening the pumping action. If this happens, doctors may try replacing the valve with either a mechanical valve or animal tissue.

## Keeping Time

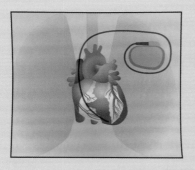

Sometimes, a person's heartbeat may become dangerously irregular, and they may be given an artificial pacemaker. This is a simple battery-powered device that senses any unsteadiness in the heartbeat and sends an electrical stimulus to the heart to get it going properly again. The pacemaker is installed just under the skin, then wired to the heart, in a minor operation.

## Heart Transplant

If heart disease is very severe, the only solution may be a heart transplant. This means the diseased heart is removed and swapped for a healthy heart from a donor who has just died. Transplants take about four hours. The new heart is stitched in and the patient is given drugs to make sure their immune system does not reject the new heart.

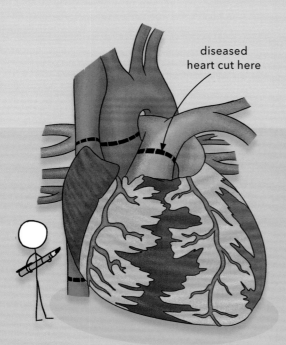

diseased
heart cut here

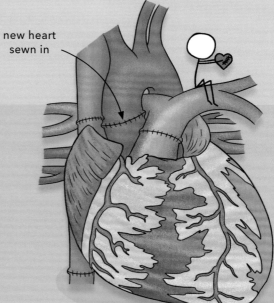

new heart
sewn in

## Heart on Ice

A patient waiting for a new heart must be on permanent standby because the transplant must be performed within a few hours of the donor dying. Once the donor's heart has been removed, it is stored in a cooler and shipped as quickly as possible to the hospital where the operation will take place.

# Staying Fit

One of the key signs of being fit and healthy is having a strong heart and lungs. That means your heart and lungs can supply your muscles with all the oxygen they need. If you get out of breath easily, it's a sign that your heart and lungs aren't fit enough.

## Hard Work!

When you exercise, your body reacts in some of the ways shown here. If you're fit and you haven't pushed too hard, your body will return to normal in just a few minutes. If you're out of shape or have really worked hard, it may take hours.

body temperature rises and you sweat

you breathe faster and deeper, taking in up to 10 times more air every minute

heart rate soars and the heart pumps more blood with each beat

the liver converts more of its stored sugar (glycogen) to glucose

blood vessels widen to increase blood flow to muscles

muscles consume up to 20 times more energy

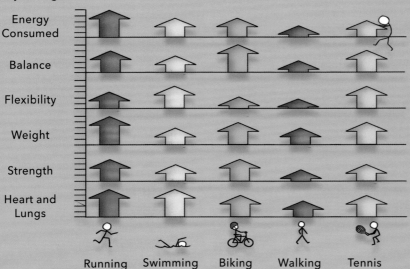

acid builds up in the muscles as they burn glucose without enough oxygen

## Exercise: What is it Good For?

Different kinds of exercise help you in different ways. Running is great for your heart and lungs but doesn't do much for flexibility. Riding a bicycle is good for muscles and for balance and coordination.

Energy Consumed

Balance

Flexibility

Weight

Strength

Heart and Lungs

Running  Swimming  Biking  Walking  Tennis

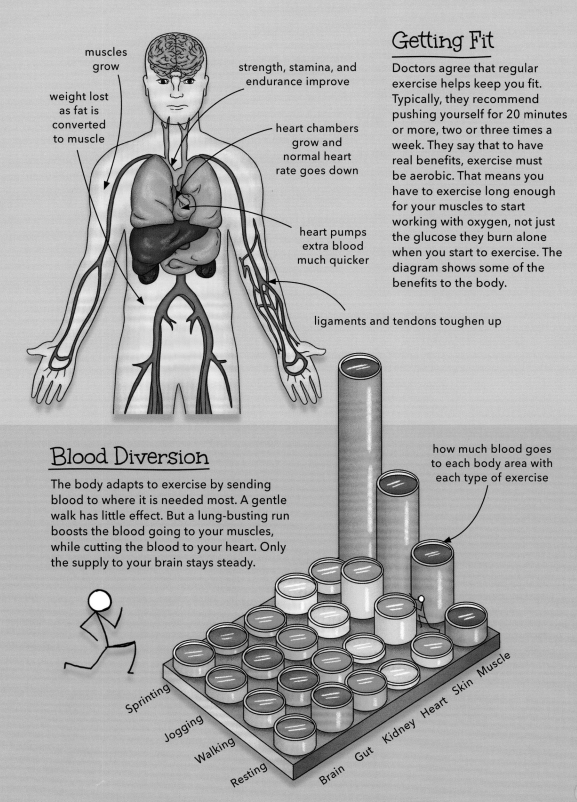

muscles grow

weight lost as fat is converted to muscle

strength, stamina, and endurance improve

heart chambers grow and normal heart rate goes down

heart pumps extra blood much quicker

ligaments and tendons toughen up

## Getting Fit

Doctors agree that regular exercise helps keep you fit. Typically, they recommend pushing yourself for 20 minutes or more, two or three times a week. They say that to have real benefits, exercise must be aerobic. That means you have to exercise long enough for your muscles to start working with oxygen, not just the glucose they burn alone when you start to exercise. The diagram shows some of the benefits to the body.

## Blood Diversion

The body adapts to exercise by sending blood to where it is needed most. A gentle walk has little effect. But a lung-busting run boosts the blood going to your muscles, while cutting the blood to your heart. Only the supply to your brain stays steady.

how much blood goes to each body area with each type of exercise

Sprinting

Jogging

Walking

Resting

Brain  Gut  Kidney  Heart  Skin  Muscle

# Speaking and Singing

Your lungs aren't just for getting air in and out of your body. They help give you a voice too. Your voice comes from the larynx, or voice box, in your throat, near the top of the airway up from your lungs. This is where your vocal cords are. They are folds of muscle stretched across the airway, leaving a small opening, called the glottis, for air.

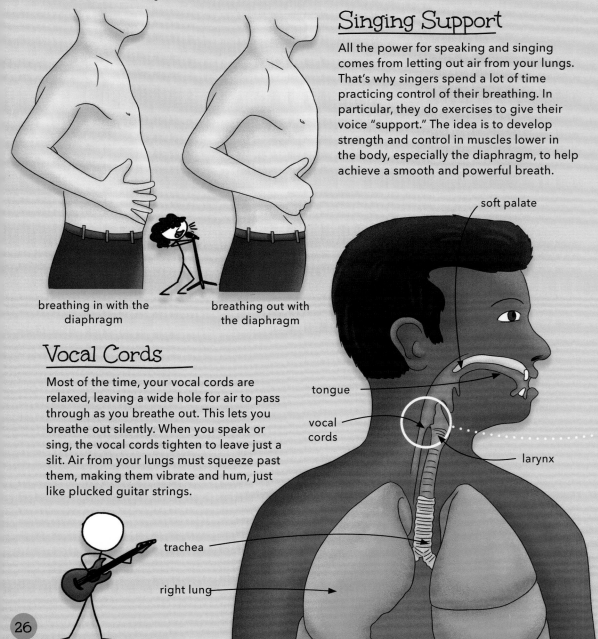

breathing in with the
diaphragm

breathing out with
the diaphragm

## Singing Support

All the power for speaking and singing comes from letting out air from your lungs. That's why singers spend a lot of time practicing control of their breathing. In particular, they do exercises to give their voice "support." The idea is to develop strength and control in muscles lower in the body, especially the diaphragm, to help achieve a smooth and powerful breath.

soft palate

## Vocal Cords

Most of the time, your vocal cords are relaxed, leaving a wide hole for air to pass through as you breathe out. This lets you breathe out silently. When you speak or sing, the vocal cords tighten to leave just a slit. Air from your lungs must squeeze past them, making them vibrate and hum, just like plucked guitar strings.

tongue

vocal
cords

larynx

trachea

right lung

## Shaping Sounds

You can only make vowel sounds—*a, e, i, o, u*—with your voice box. You have to move your lips, mouth, and tongue to change the sound to make the other letters—the choppy sounds known as consonants. This is called articulation.

Nasal *m* and *n* sounds are made by sending the sound through your nose.

Fricative sounds, such as *f, th, v,* and *z,* are made by friction. Your lips interfere with the flow of sound.

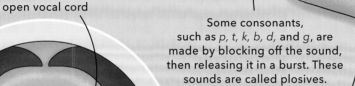

open vocal cord

Some consonants, such as *p, t, k, b, d,* and *g,* are made by blocking off the sound, then releasing it in a burst. These sounds are called plosives.

Sibilants are *s* sounds made by getting the sound to hiss through a groove in the tip of your tongue.

## Smashing Voice

Amazingly, some singers can sing so loud that they can smash glass. All glass has a resonant frequency—a speed at which it will naturally vibrate if disturbed by vibrations such as sound. If a singer hits that special frequency loud enough, the air around the glass will start shaking at the same speed, and the glass may shake itself to bits!

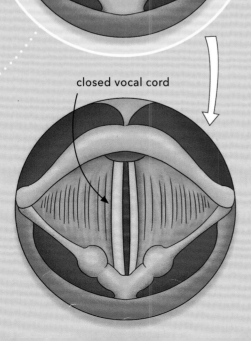

closed vocal cord

# The History of the Heart

Doctors have always known that your heart keeps you alive. But for a long time they didn't quite know how it did this. Once, they even thought your heart does your thinking, not your head! It's only since the seventeenth century, when William Harvey showed that the heart pumps blood around the body, that scientists have gradually pieced together how your heart and lungs work together to supply your body cells with fuel.

## 2000 BCE

The Ancient Egyptians believed that the heart was the key to life and morality. After a person died, they believed the heart would be weighed in the Hall of Maat, the goddess of justice. If the heart was weighed down by sin, the person would never make it to the afterlife.

2000 BCE      800      1600

## 140 CE

Like many people at the time, the Roman doctor Galen realized that the heart has valves that open and shut. He also noticed the difference between arteries and veins.

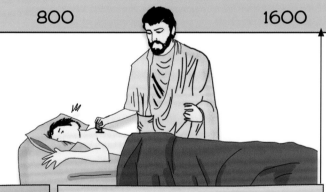

## 400 BCE

The Greek doctor Hippocrates believed the heart was the body's source of heat. In fact, more heat comes from your liver and muscles. Hippocrates also realized that the heart is linked to the lungs, and that it is a kind of pump.

## 1628

The English doctor William Harvey discovered that blood circulates continuously around the body, pumped by the heart. This was a huge discovery, and at first few people believed him. But he was right—blood goes right around the body about once every minute.

## 1774

The British scientist Joseph Priestley did some experiments to see how long a mouse could survive inside a glass jar containing a burning candle. From these and other experiments, Priestley discovered that we take in oxygen from the air when we breathe, and let out carbon dioxide.

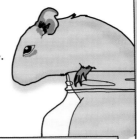

## 1925

The British doctor Henry Souttar performed surgery inside the heart, known as open-heart surgery, for the first time. He successfully corrected a defect in one of the valves in a young woman's heart. But his colleagues considered the operation too dangerous, and he was forbidden to repeat it.

## 1967

South African doctor Christiaan Barnard performed the first successful heart transplant operation. He removed a patient's diseased heart and replaced it with the healthy heart of a donor who had recently died.

1800      1900      2000

## 1818

The British doctor James Blundell carried out the first successful blood transfusion. To save a mother dying of blood loss during childbirth, he collected blood from her husband's arm and injected it with a syringe into the patient. The transfusion worked, and the mother survived.

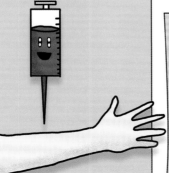

## 1944

Doctors Alfred Blalock, Helen Taussig, and Vivien Thomas at Johns Hopkins University in the United States, performed the first successful heart surgery on a baby. They corrected blue baby syndrome, in which the heart pumps too little blood, so the baby looks almost blue.

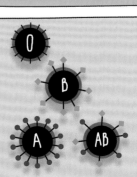

## 1901

Austrian-American doctor Karl Landsteiner discovered the four different blood groups: A, B, AB, and O. For a transfusion to work, the blood given to the patient must be of the right kind.

# More Hearty Facts

## Beat That

Your heart beats more than once every second, about 80 times a minute, and about 100,000 times every day! That means that if you live to the age of 80 or so, your heart will beat three billion times or more, without fail. Very few machines are as long-lasting and reliable as that!

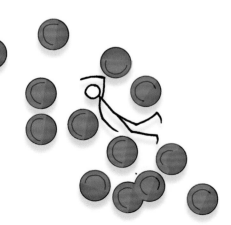

## Pumped Up

Your heart pumps about one million barrels of blood during your lifetime. That's a lot of blood—enough to fill more than 60 Olympic swimming pools. If there are 20 of you in your class at school, altogether your hearts will pump enough blood to fill ten oil supertankers.

## Cell Multitude

Your blood has to carry a lot of oxygen. So you have many more red blood cells in your body than any other kind—about 25 trillion. And because red blood cells only last about three months, your body has to make new ones at a phenomenal rate. In fact, your body makes 200 billion new red blood cells per day, not to mention 10 billion white blood cells and 400 billion platelets!

## Blood Loss

Your body makes new blood so fast you can afford to lose up to 0.3 gallons (1 L) or more before it gets really dangerous. That's why people are able to donate blood to hospitals, to use in blood transfusions. But if you lose more than 0.5 gallons (2 L) of blood, you are likely to die.

## Hot Bodies

As your body cells use energy, they release enough heat to keep you warm most of the time. In fact, they release as much heat as a 100-watt light bulb. That means if you and your 19 classmates were put together in a small room, your bodies would make as much heat as a 2-kilowatt electric heater!

## Heart Swap

About 50,000 people around the world need a heart transplant, but fewer than 5,000 actually get one because there is a shortage of suitable donor hearts. These operations are surprisingly successful. Of the people who have had a heart transplant, 90 percent survive at least a year after surgery, and more than 75 percent survive for more than three years.

# INDEX

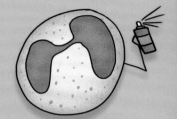

## The Author

John Farndon is Royal Literary Fellow at City&Guilds in London, United Kingdom, and the author of a huge number of books for adults and children on science, technology, and nature, including such international best sellers as *Do Not Open* and *Do You Think You're Clever?*. He has been shortlisted six times for the Royal Society's Young People's Book Prize for a science book, with titles such as *How the Earth Works*, *What Happens When?*, and *Project Body* (2016).

## The Illustrator

Venitia Dean is a freelance illustrator who grew up in Brighton, United Kingdom. She has loved drawing ever since she could hold a pencil! As a teenager she discovered a passion for figurative illustration, and when she turned nineteen she was given a digital drawing tablet for her birthday and started transferring her work to the computer. She hasn't looked back since! As well as illustration, Venitia loves reading graphic novels and walking her dog Peanut.

**Picture Credits** (abbreviations: t = top; b = bottom; c = center; l = left; r = right)
© www.shutterstock.com: 5 bl, 6 tc, 6 bl, 7 tl, 7 cr, 7 bl, 10 bc, 13 cr, 13 br, 16 cl, 16 bc, 18 cl, 21 tl, 21 br,